NSPCC happy Kids

CHILD CARE GUIDES

B ul

GW00492907

Sheila Dore

EGMONT WORLD LIMITED

"The National Society for the Prevention of Cruelty to Children (NSPCC) has a vision – a society where all children are loved, valued and able to fulfil their potential. The NSPCC is pleased to work with Egmont World Limited on the development of this series of child care guides. We believe that they will help parents and carers better understand children's and babies' needs."

Jim Harding, Chief Executive, NSPCC.

Designer: Dave Murray
Illustrator: John Haslam
Editor: Stephanie Sloan
Cover design: Craig Cameron
Front cover photograph supplied by Telegraph Colour Library

Copyright © 2000 Egmont World Limited. All rights reserved.
Published in Great Britain in 2000 by Egmont World Limited,
a division of Egmont Holding Limited,
Deanway Technology Centre, Wilmslow Road, Handforth,
Cheshire, SK9 3FB. Printed in Italy
ISBN 0 7498 4766 2
A catalogue record for this book is available
from the British Library.

Bullying

by Sheila Dore

Contents

Introduction

Bullying is still a big problem in society. It can have devastating effects on adults and children. Children who are bullied may feel trapped and powerless and too afraid to ask for help; parents whose children are bullied may worry that they are not doing enough to help.

Bullying is a difficult subject and many children needlessly suffer. The aim of this book is to help parents and carers release children from the grip of bullying.

Note:
When referrring to the child, we have alternated the use of he and she throughout the book.

CHAPTER 1
What is bullying?

Bullying can be mild or it can be extreme. It is cruel, aggressive or oppressive behaviour, usually carried out over a period of time (although there can be isolated incidents). It can be physical, such as hitting or kicking someone, or verbal, such as name-calling, or emotional, with threats and intimidation.

It may take place in full public view, or it may be hidden and unseen by others. But whenever it happens, bullying is distressing and frightening for a child, and very upsetting for parents.

Different forms of bullying
- Physical - hitting, pushing, kicking. In some cases, if a child has been seriously injured or hospitalised as a result of violent assault, bullying amounts to criminal behaviour.
- Verbal - name-calling, 'put-downs', graffiti or other written material.
- Emotional - threats and intimidation.
- Non-verbal - using threatening body language.
- Exclusion - ignoring or isolating someone.
- Undermining - constantly criticising or spreading nasty rumours.

- Racial bullying - picking on someone because of racial or ethnic differences or taunting them with remarks to do with their family, culture and ethnic background.
- Sexual harassment - sexist remarks by boys or girls or unwanted sexual attention. This can also take the form of spreading malicious rumours regarding someone's sexual reputation or threatening someone in order to extort sexual favours.
- Extortion - using threats of physical violence or malicious rumour to take food, money or other possessions, or to take advantage of someone sexually.

In some cases, bullying amounts to criminal behaviour if a child has been seriously injured or hospitalised by bullying.

The effects of bullying

Bullying can cause long-term emotional damage as well as physical scars and can affect mental and physical health. Victims of bullying are likely to feel humiliated and powerless. They may suffer a loss in confidence and self-worth, and their school work or their play may be disrupted. The effects can sometimes last into adulthood. At its worst, bullying has driven victims to self-harm and suicide.

Who bullies?

Bullying may be carried out by one person or by a whole group of people. A person who bullies is likely to be older, or bigger in size than their victim, or with some other advantage, such as strength in numbers, because this gives them a sense of power. The stereotype of a bully is a vicious thug, and while this sort of bully exists, there are many other types of bully. Girls bully as well as boys, and sometimes bullies are smart, clever people who are sly and who know how to manipulate others. Adults as well as children are capable of bullying.

Why bully?

People who bully may feel powerless and deeply unhappy inside, and their bullying behaviour gives them a feeling of power and allows them to take out their pent-up feelings on others. They may not be conscious of their motives; they may not even realise the effect their behaviour is having on others. They may have had a violent upbringing, where aggression is the only thing they know. They may be people who have always been used to getting their own way. Or they may themselves be victims of bullying or abuse. Whatever the reasons, and whatever help such a person might need, their bullying behaviour should not be tolerated.

Who are the victims?

Anyone of any age can become a victim of bullying. One child might be bullied for being 'stupid' or 'fat', another for being 'brainy' or 'scrawny'. One might be bullied for being rich and 'stuck up', another for being 'scruffy' and poor. The point is that someone who bullies will find an excuse to pick on the other person. This could be an obvious difference, such as size, or wearing glasses, or a different accent, or it could be an imagined difference, such as believing their victim to be inferior in some way. A victim may be someone who is constantly targeted, or someone who just happens to be in the wrong place at the wrong time. Some victims seem to attract negative attention wherever they go; others, however, may be generally happy-go-lucky children whose only weakness lies in being too 'nice' - that is, they are unused to dealing with such aggressive behaviour and may be easily upset. Crying, or showing you're upset, is exactly the response the bully wants.

Where does bullying happen?

Bullying mainly occurs in schools. Unfortunately, bullying is still rife in all kinds of schools:

- state schools, independent or public school, day or boarding school;
- primary, secondary, even nursery school;
- it can happen in the classroom, in the playground, toilets or corridors, usually out of sight of teachers or supervisors.

Bullying also happens in public institutions, in the workplace, in communities or at home.

Adults as well as children can be victims of bullying. Sadly, bullying is still a big problem in society.

Take it seriously

The idea that bullying is a 'normal' part of life, or that it helps 'toughen' someone up, is recognised nowadays as a myth. Many adults who were bullied as children talk about the trauma and distress it caused them and say that what made it even worse was that there was no one to turn to for help. Fortunately, the climate is changing. We owe it to ourselves and our children to take any incidents of bullying seriously. Whatever the reasons for bullying, it is not acceptable behaviour.

CHAPTER 2

Is my child being bullied?

It can be hard for parents to know whether or not a child is being bullied. One of the reasons for this is that a child may be too frightened to tell anyone, in case the bullying gets worse. Or, she may be so beaten down by the bullying that she even believes that, in some way, she deserves it. Another reason is that, if bullying is non-physical, there may be no outward signs.

Warning signs

- Physical injury - swelling or bruises or red marks or cuts; if injuries are serious, seek medical help.
- Damage to personal property - clothes may be torn, toys or school equipment broken.
- The child is over-tired and hungry from not eating lunch (if his school-dinner money or packed lunch has been stolen by bullies).
- The child is afraid to go to school, or mysteriously 'ill' every morning (even though illness may be faked, a child may suffer actual ill health because of bullying).

- The child asks for money or steals money (to pay bullies).
- The child is afraid of travelling on the school bus or on her own to school.
- The child displays nervous symptoms and loss of confidence, or generally seems distressed.
- The child stops eating or sleeping or has nightmares.
- The child attempts self-harm or threatens suicide.
- The child begins to bully others.
- The child truants from school.
- The child refuses to say what's wrong.
- The child is generally withdrawn.

It is also possible for a child to be bullied without displaying any of these symptoms.

Stop and think

Try to avoid over-reacting if your child displays any of these signs. There may be other reasons for these symptoms - for example, children are often tired and hungry when they come home from school, and it is very normal for teenagers to want to withdraw and spend a lot of time in their room. So, it is vital to stay calm and assess the situation carefully before jumping to any conclusions about bullying. If your child is being bullied, it is likely to be an extremely delicate situation getting him or her to talk about it.

Ask the child directly

The first approach is to sit down quietly with the child and ask if she is having a problem with bullying. This is usually better than screaming hysterically or saying, in an accusing voice, 'you're being bullied, aren't you?' which tends to make a child clam up. Let the child know how you feel; say 'I'm worried about you', or 'I'm feeling concerned that you might be being bullied. Bullying is a serious problem and I want to help.'

If the child denies that there is any problem, or doesn't even want to talk about it, let her know that you are willing to listen - any time of day or night - if and when she is ready to talk. (It may be that she is not being bullied but something else is bothering her.) In the meantime, it is important for parents to be vigilant, because a child who is being bullied may feel so hopeless that she may attempt something drastic such as taking an overdose or running away from home. Take any such threats seriously, and seek professional help if necessary. You could do this by talking to your GP, who may refer the child to counselling, or by talking to your local council's Education Welfare Officer.

Name the problem

Sometimes children are suffering without realising that what they are experiencing is bullying. For example, your child may have been a victim of name-calling for months and made to feel a 'wimp' for getting upset about a bit of 'fun'. So, by putting a name to it – i.e. by actually calling it bullying – you make it easier for a child to talk about it.

However, one of the things that make it hard for children to talk about bullying is the fear of what might happen to them if they tell.

CHAPTER 3

To tell or not to tell

'Don't tell' - that is the dilemma for most people who are being bullied. They have been given a strong message that if they tell anyone, the bullying will get worse. They may be terrified of what will happen to them. Or they may be scared that people will think that they are making things up and laugh at them. One of the reasons that bullying has such a hold is because the fear of telling is part of the bullying; it is part of the intimidation. Bullying, like other forms of abuse, is usually carried out in an air of secrecy.

Why children are afraid to tell

- They fear the bullying may get worse; including other friends or family members being bullied.

- They may be laughed at, or not taken seriously, thus adding to feelings of humiliation.

- They may feel so hopeless that they feel nothing can be done about it anyway.

- They may fear attracting too much attention or a full-scale drama: parents going up to the school, for example, and creating a 'scene'.

- They may feel ashamed of being bullied and guilty about not being able to deal with it themselves.
- They may feel guilty at having witnessed bullying and not done anything about it (perhaps they were too scared that the bullies might turn on them).
- They may not want to upset their parents, or may fear that their parents may be angry with them.

Talking to a child

If you know, or suspect your child is being bullied, and they refuse to talk about it, let them know that you are willing to listen to them any time of day or night, whenever they feel ready to talk. Say you understand how scary bullying is, and how hard it can be to talk about it. Say that you care about them and don't want them to be hurt. Give them reasons why it is OK to break the taboo of silence. (It may be that you, too, had the 'Don't Tell' message strongly ingrained into you during your own childhood, in which case, make sure that you, too understand the following points.)

Breaking the code of silence

- Let a child know that by not talking about bullying he is giving the bully even more power. Asking for help is different from 'grassing people up'. If he doesn't want to talk to you about it, suggest someone else he could turn to for help - a teacher, or a relative or friend whom they trust, for example.

- Spell out to a child that no one deserves to be bullied and that he, and everyone else, has a right to be treated with respect. Bullying is abusive behaviour and he should not have to put up with it.

- Tell him that he has a right to help and that

help is available, and if you know what is going on you can get help (if a young child), or decide together on the best way of getting help (if an older child). Say that providing protection (after telling about the bullying) is part of getting help.

• Say that you do not believe he should sort it out on his own. Some problems, like bullying, often need adult intervention. Depending on the age of the child, ask what he thinks should be done about it. He may welcome a suggestion from you of going to talk to the school. Teenagers, on the other hand, may want to talk to a teacher themselves, without you; say that you understand, and are willing to support them in whatever way they want you to.

- Let your child know that you know how much suffering bullying can cause and that you do not want him to suffer on his own.

- Say that it may not be just his problem, but something that is affecting other people in the school, in which case he should not carry the burden of responsibility on his shoulders. It may be the school's problem or a community problem.

CHAPTER 4

Helping a child who is bullied

If you know your child is being bullied, you can help, either by taking the matter further or talking to the child about how to deal with the situation (see Chapter 7, 'Dealing with bullying') .

Before taking any action, it is important that you gain as much information as possible so that you can assess the scale of the problem. Discuss the situation with your child, and possibly other children or other parents, and assess the emotional and physical state of your child. Obviously, the more distressed or injured a child is, the more urgent need there is to act. If the bullying seems 'mild', on the other hand, it may be that you can help your child learn strategies for dealing with it. But be careful that what seems mild to you may still feel deeply distressing to a child. However major or minor the bullying, the chances are that your child will need a lot of emotional support.

Do	**Don't**
Reassure the child that, now he has told you about being bullied, you will help him get protection from further bullying.	Ignore the problem.
	Rush off to find the culprits and 'sort them out'.
Seek medical attention if necessary. Keep written notes of any incidents, in case you decide to take further action.	Tell the child to 'fight back'. (He obviously feels powerless to do that or he would not be bullied.)
If there is no serious physical injury, assess the situation before taking any action; then if necessary contact the school or other authorities.	Press the child for too much information all at once.
	Fly into a rage or hysterics, however angry or upset you may be feeling.
Be patient with the child and wait till she is ready to talk.	Make your child feel bad or ashamed for being bullied.
Try to stay calm while talking to the child.	Assume that your child's story is the only version of events.
Let the child know how you feel by saying 'I'm very worried' or 'I'm upset'.	

Other ways to help the child

- Be patient and listen to what a child has to say. Time and again, adults who were bullied as children say that what would have helped them most would have been if an adult had listened to them and taken them seriously.

- Depending on the age of the child, ask what help they think they need and discuss what should be done about the bullying. If a very young child, tell her clearly what you intend to do about it, and why. For example, say 'I'm going to talk to the play-leader and ask him to stop Jo hitting you'.

- Get the facts if possible; find out who else is involved; perhaps by telephoning another parent whom you trust. (Avoid phoning parents whom you don't know or trust, as this may cause more trouble.)

- Help a child to be aware of personal safety and how to minimise the risks - for example, by avoiding walking alone to school or not taking valuable possessions into school.

- There may be other things bothering your child, and, if so, being bullied could be a symptom of her feeling unsettled or unsure of herself or vulnerable. Give her opportunities to talk about what else is going on. She may need extra attention or support from you if she has recently changed school, for example, or is adjusting to a changed family situation.

- If a child doesn't want to talk about it, try to be patient and let her open up in her own good time. Forcing a child to talk, or keeping the focus on her the whole time, may make her feel even more miserable. Give her lots of affection and try to carry on with normal life.

- Do things to help rebuild your child's self-esteem, such as showing her your appreciation and helping her feel accepted and valued. Encourage her to take up new interests and activities which will help build her confidence. This could include going to self-defence classes, which as well as teaching skills, are very good for developing confidence.

CHAPTER 5

Talking to the school

If your child is being bullied at school and you have discussed the options with your child, you will probably decide to talk to the school in an attempt to have the bullying stopped. All schools have a responsibility to protect pupils from bullying. However, how the school will respond depends a great deal on the staff, the atmosphere in the school and the school's anti-bullying policy. Most schools have an anti-bullying policy, but some schools are more effective than others in carrying it out.

Step by step

- Arrange to see the class teacher.
- Take a notebook to jot down the main points of what is said at the meeting.
- Make it clear that you will not tolerate bullying, and tell the teacher what effect it is having on your child.
- Ask for protection for your child by:

  1) asking the teacher for confidentiality in order to protect your child from any recriminations from the bully for 'telling'. Now that the school has been alerted members of staff could keep an eye out for any bullying.

2) asking for adequate supervision of play areas and extra supervision if necessary.

- Ask how the school intends to deal with the bullies and the bullying.
- Ask what action is proposed, and ask for a date by which it will happen.
- Follow up to see what progress has been made.
- If you are unsatisfied by the teacher's response, take the matter to the headteacher.
- If you are still not satisfied, write to the chair of the school governors.

Do	Don't
Make an appointment to see the class teacher.	Go marching into the school and cause a scene.
Try to stay calm, even though you may be feeling very angry and upset.	Lose your temper with the teacher - she or he is more likely to want to help you if you are calm and rational.
Listen to what the teacher has to say, even if you don't agree. It's important to establish a dialogue, and you are more likely to get your point of view listened to as well.	Rant and rave in a monologue, telling the teacher everything you think is wrong with the school.
Set a good example to your child of how to stand up for your rights and deal with problems in a constructive way.	Turn it into a major drama.

Expect change overnight. |
| Allow time for the situation to change. | |

Is your child a bully?

You may have been summoned to the school because of allegations that your child is a bully. Follow the same Dos and Don'ts in communicating with the teacher (see Chapter 8, Is my child a bully?).

What about teacher bullies?

Some teachers have been known to bully pupils or pick on them in an unfair way. This is a difficult situation for parents to deal with, especially if the teacher denies there is a problem. If possible, take the matter up with the teacher in the first instance, but, again, follow the Dos and Don'ts, and take the matter to the head teacher if necessary. Sometimes teachers themselves are being bullied.

Legal responsibility

Anti-bullying policies are not a legal requirement in schools, but they are a government recommendation. However, schools have a duty of care towards your child. If your child's education is being disrupted by bullying, you have a right to tell the school that you believe it is failing in its duty of care. If necessary, you can even threaten legal action.

Ideally, a school will take any allegations of bullying very seriously and make sure that something is done about it. However, you may encounter a negative response, such as a denial that there's a problem - the child is just 'imagining' it. Sometimes it is hard to convince anyone that bullying is taking place, because so much of it is undercover. A teacher might not believe that so-and-so is capable of bullying - "but he never causes any trouble ...". Or they may even deny that any bullying goes on in the school. If so, you may need to take further action.

CHAPTER 6

Where else to get help

If you are not satisfied with the school's response, or if your child is being bullied somewhere other than school, you will probably need to seek help elsewhere.

Taking further action at school

- If you are dissatisfied with the school's response, contact the chair of the school governors (the school can tell you how to do this). Bullying can affect the whole school community and, if you believe there is a problem, you may want to enrol the support of other parents to have something done about it.

- Depending on the gravity of the situation, consider keeping your child off school till the bullying is stopped. (Talk to the Council's Education Welfare Officer about this.)

- Ask the school to organise an anti-bullying workshop run by experts in anti-bullying (see helplist). These workshops help to reduce prejudice and aggression.

- Seek legal advice if necessary (see helplist).

- If you are still not happy with the outcome, you could approach your LEA (Local Education

Authority). You could write to your MP about it. You could even sue the school. However, consider very carefully how much energy or time you are able to put into a long, drawn-out and painful campaign. Sometimes - especially if it seems a losing battle and the school refuses to act or seems at a loss as to how to deal with the bullying - it is easier, on yourself and the child, to transfer your child to another school where she can peacefully get on with her education.

Changing school

This can be a hard decision to make, so talk to your child about the possibilities and discuss the pros and cons with her. Although changing school can be a big adjustment at first, many children thrive in new surroundings and settle down to their studies and make new friends. When choosing a school, be sure to check on the school's approach to bullying.

• As an alternative, you might want to consider educating your child at home. This option works well for many children and parents; however, it requires commitment, time and dedication. If you decide on home education, it is advisable to be part of a network with other parents and children so that your child does not become too isolated (see helplist).

Your child is bullied away from school

If your child is bullied in the community, or on the way to or from school, the school may be able to offer some help but does not have a legal responsibility outside the school grounds.

• It may be wise for you to arrange for your child to be accompanied by an adult or other (trusted) children, or to arrange alternative transport for the child.
• Report any serious assault, or threat of serious assault, to the police, who may decide to prosecute (if the perpetrators are over ten years of age). You would need to provide evidence of any assault or threat; keep any medical notes as well as a written record of events.

- Talk to the Police Community Liaison Officer. Even if it is not a serious assault, the police may be able to keep a lookout or step up their presence in the area. Police response varies greatly depending on the circumstances and the local area. (Reporting bullying to the police can sometimes carry a risk of recriminations by a bullying gang. Depending on the climate, you may have to weigh up the exercising of your rights with the safest way to protect your family. Occasionally, families decide to move home because, although this may seem to be giving the bullies power, it feels too big a problem to tackle and they have to put the welfare of the family first.)
- Racial bullying, whether in or away from school, cannot be tolerated. There is now more awareness within the police and other authorities (education, health, social services) of racism, and much is being done to help prevent it.
- Take similar steps to those outlined above and also talk to leaders of your local ethnic community.

Who else can help the child?

- The child could phone ChildLine (see helplist) or talk to a mentor. Some schools now have student counsellors or mentors whom children can talk to about things that are bothering them. Or, you and your child may be able to think of someone else – perhaps a trusted friend or relative – whom your child may find it easier to talk to.

- Talk to the Council's Education Welfare Officer.
- Seek professional counselling through your GP or through the school or Education Welfare or Youth Services.
- The Children's Legal Centre provides free legal advice regarding children and the law.

- Kidscape is a charity set up to prevent bullying and abuse. It has a helpline for parents of bullied or bullying children.

Contact addresses for these, and helplines, are listed at the end of this book.

Dealing with bullying can be disruptive to home and family life. As well as helping the child, it is important that you get help for yourself. (See Chapter 9, 'Getting support for yourself'.)

CHAPTER 7

Dealing with bullying

Generally speaking, children should not be left to sort out a bullying problem on their own. However, parents can give additional help to children by suggesting ways of dealing with the bullying behaviour, especially if it is not too severe. (If a child is seriously at risk, keep him off school or away from wherever the bullying happened, e.g. park or route he walks from school.) It is also useful for parents to have a few tips for dealing with the bullying behaviour of children - other people's or their own.

Helping children deal with bullying

- Encourage a child to try to walk away, or stay in a group, as he is less likely to be picked on with other people around. He may need your help in making new friends.

- Make sure a child knows who to ask for help and that he has a right to ask for help. At school, this means a teacher, supervisor, playground leader or school counsellor. If not at school, he should ask another parent or adult. Talk about possible scenarios with your child and decide together who would be the best person to ask for help in each situation.

- Help a child learn assertiveness skills, especially if he has a tendency to be too compliant. Help him learn to shout 'No!' if necessary, and to walk purposefully and confidently (he can practise at home.)

- You and your child could talk about what to do in different situations, and act some of these out in a 'role play', so that he has a chance to practise saying the right words. For example, in response to name-calling, saying firmly 'No, I am not stupid', or, 'Just because I wear glasses doesn't mean I have four eyes'.

- Encourage a child to try to hide his feelings so that the bullies cannot see that he's upset or angry. If he practises staying calm and 'neutral' and looking bored, he is less likely to be bullied.

- Encourage him to talk about his feelings at home, where he feels safe. Let him write about his feelings or draw pictures; this is a good way of dealing with painful emotions.

- A child may feel bullied at home. Differentiate between bullying and a 'scrap' between brothers and sisters.

- Do what you can to help your child rebuild his self-esteem. This means giving him opportunities to do things that help him build his confidence and feel good about himself, e.g. asking for help with simple household tasks. It also means showing him you care and accepting him just the way he is, without putting any pressure on him.

- If your child has a long-term tendency to be a victim, he may have learned from an early age that being bullied is a way of getting attention. Seek professional help, if necessary, from child-counselling services or family therapy (see helplist) to help him change his 'victim' pattern of behaviour.

Name-calling

- Help children differentiate between name-calling and teasing. Teasing is acceptable only when it is humorous.

- Help children learn to ignore name-calling.

- If your child seems over-sensitive, help him learn not to react to everything. He is more likely to be a target to bullies that way. Help him develop a sense of humour and the art of banter.

- Your child may have an annoying habit or condition (such as body odour) which really does offend other children. If so, the name calling may be the children's way of giving him feedback and he may need help in correcting his anti-social behaviour.

Dealing with bullying behaviour in children

- Tell a child that bullying is unacceptable, and wherever possible, nip it in the bud at an early age. With young children, sometimes just holding the child firmly and saying 'No' quietly but clearly and firmly helps a child learn that hurting others is not allowed. Patterns of bullying behaviour often start at an early age.

- Talk assertively to the child (your own or someone else's), saying 'I feel very angry when you do that.' Or simply name the behaviour: 'You're bullying. Please stop that.' Or 'we don't hit in this house.' Avoid hitting a child, as it gives a message that hitting is OK.

- If you see bullying in the street, either intervene as appropriate (depending on the ages of the children and your own personal safety in the situation) or get help or shout 'Oi!' to let the bullies know that you have seen them. (Only intervene verbally, without resorting to violence, otherwise you could face a charge of assault to a child.) If necessary, call the police or the NSPCC 24-hour helpline. You could also report the incident to the school (if you can identify which school they go to).

- Avoid giving a child attention only when they are bullying or being naughty, because the child learns that this is the best way to get attention.

Dealing with bullying behaviour in adults

- If you are being bullied at work or at home, or even by your children, you need to get support for yourself (see Chapter 9, Getting support for yourself and 'Where can I go for Help').

CHAPTER 8
Is my child a bully?

You may have an idea that your child has been bullying, or you may be shocked to be told that your child is a 'bully'.

- Take any allegations seriously. Check the facts. Listen to your child's side of the story before doing anything else. (You may then want to check other versions of events.) There may be wrongful allegations about her behaviour, or, if she admits to bullying, she may have what she thinks is a plausible reason. Or, she may not be aware that anything is wrong.

- Tell your child that, whatever the reasons, and whether or not she agrees it is bullying, the bullying behaviour is unacceptable and must be stopped immediately. You want her to take full responsibility for her behaviour.

- If she thinks she is being unfairly blamed for bullying, she may need your support in presenting her case to the school, or, in more serious cases, to the police. Whether or not the accusations are true, she may need legal advice or the support of an advocacy service (see helplist).

- Try to stay calm and clear-headed. If you are

feeling upset or angry, tell the child how you feel. However, avoid humiliating the child or calling her a 'bully' - this just makes communication more difficult. Say you still love her; it is just her bullying behaviour that has to change.

• Ask your child how she thinks the bullying could best be stopped. For example, if there are others involved and she is under pressure from a group, she might need support from you in talking to the school (see 'To tell or not to tell' and 'Talking to the school' chapters).

- If your child has been bullying, tell her that you will do everything in your power to help her change her behaviour.
- Sometimes, the child who bullies is the child who needs the most help of all. Bullying, and other destructive behaviour, can be a symptom of distress, disturbing thoughts or some deep underlying need that is not being met. (Research has shown that children who bully are at more risk of suicide than children who are bullied.)

Helping a child change behaviour

If a child has been bullying, she is probably in need of some kind of help, either emotional support or practical help in managing her behaviour. She may also need help in dealing with unfair treatment - i.e. having bullied in the past, does she still get the blame for everything?

- Listen to your child, and see if you can find out the underlying causes of her behaviour. She may be being bullied herself or having problems at school, or be troubled about things at home. Ask how you can help her. You may need to support her in getting her educational needs properly met. She may feel frustrated if she is experiencing difficulty in learning - she may be dyslexic, for example, and need extra learning support. She may have a high level of ability and is feeling held back. Or she may need to talk about whatever is going on in the family. If there are things that are bothering you, be honest and bring them out into the open (see next chapter, 'Getting support for yourself').

- Give her the chance to talk about how she is feeling. Bullying is sometimes an outlet for bottled-up emotions. She may also need help in finding another outlet for her emotions, such as sport, music, drama, painting or writing a journal. Self-expression is sometimes the key.

- Help your child learn how to resist taunts and provocation. He may get into trouble because he loses his temper with other children, even though they 'started it'.

- Help your child understand the effect that bullying behaviour has on her victim. Help her develop empathy and respect for other people's feelings. Adults who bullied as children often say they had 'no idea at the time' of the effect their behaviour had on their victims.

- If bullying is a way of getting attention, help your child learn more useful ways to get noticed, and pay attention to her when her behaviour is positive, rather than negative.

- Impose sanctions, if necessary, such as being 'grounded' or withdrawal of privileges if the bullying continues. Agree on possible rewards for good behaviour.

- It could take time for her to change patterns of behaviour. Set realistic goals, and monitor and discuss progress. If you suspect your child has a behaviour disorder, seek professional help (see helplist).

- If bullying makes your child feel powerful, and

helps her feel the leader of the group, give her opportunities to develop leadership skills in more constructive ways - for example, through team sport.

- If she is hanging out with the 'wrong crowd', help her take up new interests and activities and make new friends.

- If necessary, try to reduce stress or aggression in the home. Try to be positive and supportive to your child. A child who feels persecuted is more likely to resort to bullying.

- Help her build her self-esteem and confidence by showing your appreciation of her and giving her the chance to do things that she can achieve and feel good about.

CHAPTER 9

Getting support for yourself

For parents, as well as children, dealing with bullying can be difficult, stressful and exhausting. It can take its toll on all family members. Whether you are helping a child who has been bullied, or helping a child change his bullying behaviour, you are probably giving the child a lot of attention and support and, in turn, it is important that you get support for yourself.

- Practise relaxation techniques that help you calm down; or do some kind of activity that you find therapeutic - for example, sport or yoga. Even though, as a busy parent, you might think 'I haven't got time for any of that', it's worth seeing if you can somehow make a little bit of time every day or every week. Make it a priority - your own sanity and well-being are important.

- Talk to someone about the problems you are facing - not just about bullying but life issues, such as bereavement, separation, family change. This could be to a friend or a relative or your partner if you have one. Or you could ring one of the excellent helplines listed at the end of the book. Sometimes, just 'getting things off your chest' can stop you bottling up feelings and help preserve your sanity.

- If you are facing serious problems, such as domestic violence or drug or alcohol addiction, talk to a helpline, doctor or counsellor, who will be able to refer you to a range of services available. You will be helping yourself and your children in the long run.

- Keep your batteries charged by taking 'time out' from the children if possible and doing things you enjoy. (Even half an hour a day or a few hours a week can make all the difference.) This helps to take some of the strain off and keeps things in perspective, and takes some of the focus off the child.

- Allow time to recover from the trauma of bullying. If you were bullied or abused as a child, you may have some deeply painful feelings that have come to the surface again through the bullying of your child. Seek the help of a professional counsellor. This will help the healing process, and will also help you to separate your own issues from those of your child.

- Consider joining a parenting course, where you meet other parents and learn useful strategies and skills.

- Keep an open attitude, and be willing to adjust your parenting style if necessary. For example, are you too strict or do you push your child? Are you aggressive with him, or are you too passive? Are you a victim yourself? Do you need to let go of the reins a bit or take a firmer hold?

- If you yourself are being bullied, by a child or a teenager or at work, take steps to address the issue. Remember the first step is naming the problem. The second step is getting help.

- By asking for help with your problems, you are setting an excellent example to your child that it is OK to ask for help.

CHAPTER 10

Preventing bullying

It takes time and effort to stop bullying. But the best strategy of all is to prevent it happening in the first place.

- Set clear limits on children's behaviour. Children need to know from an early age (toddlers upwards) that 'No' means no. Bullying behaviour is not acceptable, and hurting people is not the way to get their needs met. Help children learn to express their needs in positive ways.

- The more children's basic needs are met - for example, positive attention, love, care and affection as well as educational needs - the less likely they are to resort to bullying behaviour.

- Listen to what children have to say, and give them the chance to talk about their feelings. The more children feel understood and heard, the more confidence and self-esteem they will have and the less they will bottle up their emotions.

- Help build children's self-esteem by showing your appreciation of them, taking an interest and noticing when they're kind or praising them for their achievements, however large or small.

- Try not to give children attention only when they're being 'naughty'. This can set up negative behaviour patterns early in childhood. Children usually prefer negative attention than no attention at all.

- Help children and teenagers be aware of the risks of bullying and how to keep safe.

- Help children overcome their prejudices about race or gender or disability; schools as well as parents have a responsibility to do this.

- Learn to manage your own behaviour as

parents so that you set a good example to your children. This may mean learning assertiveness skills rather than being too passive or using aggression.

- Applaud and support the excellent work that is being done around the country to help overcome bullying. Schools that have been successful in drastically reducing levels of bullying have generally involved staff and pupils in finding solutions.

Conclusion

Bullying is a social menace. If we see it as something not just for parents to sort out but as a whole community issue, we can work together towards solving the problem for ourselves, our children, and, eventually, their children.

Where can I go for help?

Helplines
Advisory Centre for Education (ACE)
Tel: 020 7354 8321 (Mon to Fri, 2-5pm)
Free advice and publications about education law.

The Anti-bullying Campaign
185 Tower Bridge Road
London SE1 2UF

Tel: 020 7378 1446 (Mon to Fri, 10am-4pm)
Helpline for children and parents concerned
about bullying.

ChildLine
Tel: 0800 1111

ChildLine is the free, national, 24-hour helpline for
any child or young person with any problem.
Trained volunteer counsellors comfort, advise and
protect children and young people.

Practical leaflets on bullying (for both children and
parents) are available from ChildLine, Freepost
1111, London N1 0BR or from the website on
www.childline.org.uk

Children's Legal Centre

Tel: 01206 873 820 (Mon to Fri, 2-5pm)
e-mail clc@essex.ac.uk
website: www2.essex.ac.uk/clc/

Provides free legal advice regarding children and the law. They have a leaflet available regarding bullying and the law.

Kidscape

2 Grosvenor Gardens
London SW1W ODH

Tel: 020 7730 3300 (Mon to Fri, 10am to 4pm)

Charity to prevent bullying and abuse. Helpline for parents of bullied or bullying children. Send A4 SAE for free Bullying Information Pack.

NSPCC

NSPCC National Centre
42 Curtain Road
London EC2A 3NH
Website: www.nspcc.org.uk
The National Society for the Prevention of Cruelty to Children (NSPCC) is the UK's leading charity specialising in child protection and the prevention of cruelty to children. It also operates the NSPCC Child Protection Helpline – a free, 24-hour service which provides counselling, information and advice to anyone concerned about a child at risk of abuse. The Helpline number is: 0808 800 5000
Textphone: 0800 056 0566

Parentline Plus

Highgate Studios
53-79 Highgate Road
Kentish Town
London NW5 1TL

Tel: 0808 800 2222
Textphone: 0800 783 6783
Website: www.parentlineplus.org.uk

Incorporates the 'Parentline' freephone helpline which offers support and information for anyone in a parenting role. It also offers a variety of services, including parenting courses.

Young Minds (The National Association for Child and Family Mental Health)

Tel: 0800 018 2138 (Mon and Fri, 10am-1pm, Tues-Thurs 1pm-4pm)

A telephone service providing information and advice for anyone with concerns about the mental health of a child or young person.

Samaritans

Tel: 0345 909090

24-hour helpline for anyone with problems.

Counselling
Youth Access

1A Taylor's Yard
67 Alderbrook Road
London SW12 8AD
Tel: 020 8772 9900

Provides names and addresses of local free counselling services to young people.

Family Service Units

207 Old Marylebone Road
London NW1 5QP
Tel: 020 7402 5175

Provides family counselling and support in branches throughout England. Ring to obtain number of your local branch.

Home education

Association of British Correspondence Colleges

PO Box 17926
London SW19 3WB
Tel: 020 8544 9559

Provides correspondence courses for young people wishing to do GCSEs and A levels.

Mercers College

Tel: 01920 465 926

Provides correspondence courses for children from nursery school age upwards.

Home Education Advisory Service

PO Box 98
Welwyn Garden City
Herts
AL8 6AN

Provides support for children to help get them back into the local education system. Send large SAE for comprehensive information pack.

Other useful contacts
National Association for the Gifted Child

Elder House
540 Elder Gate
Milton Keynes MK9 1LR
Helpline for parents: 01908 673677
Youth helpline: 01908 698498
email nagc@rmplc.co.uk

Taking into account the needs of gifted children.

Home-Start UK

2 Salisbury Road
Leicester LE1 7QR
Tel: 0116 233 9955

Volunteers offer support, friendship and practical help to young families in their own homes. There are schemes throughout the UK.

Commission for Racial Equality (CRE)

Elliot House
10-12 Allington Street
London SW1E 5HE
Tel: 020 7828 7022

An independent organisation that exists to tackle racial discrimination and promote racial equality. It works to encourage fair treatment and to promote equal opportunities for everyone, regardless of their race, colour, nationality, or national or ethnic origin. It provides information and advice to people who think they have suffered racial discrimination or harrassment.

Council for Disabled Children

5 Wakley Street
London EC1V QE
Tel: 020 7843 6061/6058

Provides an information and advice service on all matters relating to disability, children and their families.

National Coalition Building Institute (NCBI)

PO Box 411
Leicester LE4 8ZY
Tel: 0116 260 3232

Workshops on Ending Bullying in Schools, Conflict Resolution and Prejudice Reduction.

National Council for One Parent Families

255 Kentish Town Road
London NW5 2LX
Tel: 020 7267 1361
Lone Parent Line: 0800 018 5026
Maintenance & Money Line: 0207 428 5428
(Mon and Fri, 10.30am-1.30pm,
Wed 3-6pm)
Information service for lone parents.

Scottish Child Law Centre

Lion Chambers
170 Hope Street
Glasgow G2 2TU
Tel: 0141 226 3434 (Tues-Fri, 10am-4pm)

Provides free legal advice about children and Scottish law.

Anti-bullying policy information

A report on schools' anti-bullying policies is now obtainable on the Internet, at

www.ofsted.gov.uk

We hope you enjoyed reading this book and would like to read other titles in the NSPCC range. If you have any difficulty finding other titles you can order them direct (p&p is free) from Egmont World Limited, P O Box 7, Manchester M19 2HD. Please make a cheque payable to Egmont World Limited and list the titles(s) you want to order on a separate piece of paper.

Please don't forget to include your address and postcode.

Thank you

… and remember every book purchased means another contribution towards the NSPCC cause.

NSPCC Child Care Guides   £2.99

First-time Parent,
by Faye Corlett   0 7498 4669 0

Understanding Your Baby,
by Eileen Hayes   0 7498 46704

Understanding Your Toddler,
by Eileen Hayes   0 7498 4671 2

Toddler Talk and Learning,
by Ken Adams   0 7498 4776 X

Sleeping Through the Night,
by Faye Corlett   0 7498 4775 1

Bullying,
by Sheila Dore   0 7498 4766 2

A Special Child in the Family,
by Mal Leicester   0 7498 4673 9

Being Different,
by Mal Leicester   0 7498 4765 4

Potty Training and Child Development,
by Faye Corlett   0 7498 4763 8

Changing Families,
by Sheila Dore   0 7498 4762 X

Positive Parenting,
by Eileen Hayes   0 7498 4674 7

Bedtimes and Mealtimes,
by Margaret Bamforth   0 7498 4672 0

NSPCC Learning Guides   **£2.99**
by Nicola Morgan

Get Ready for School   0 7498 4492 2

Reading and Writing at School 0 7498 4491 4

NSPCC Happy Kids Story Books **£2.99**
by Michaela Morgan

Maya and the New Baby.   0 7498 4637 2

Spike and the Footy Shirt   0 7498 4636 4

Jordan and the Different Day   0 7498 4638 0

Jody and the Biscuit Bully   0 7498 4635 6

Emily and the Stranger   0 7498 4639 9

Happy Kids All Together Now   0 7498 4640 2